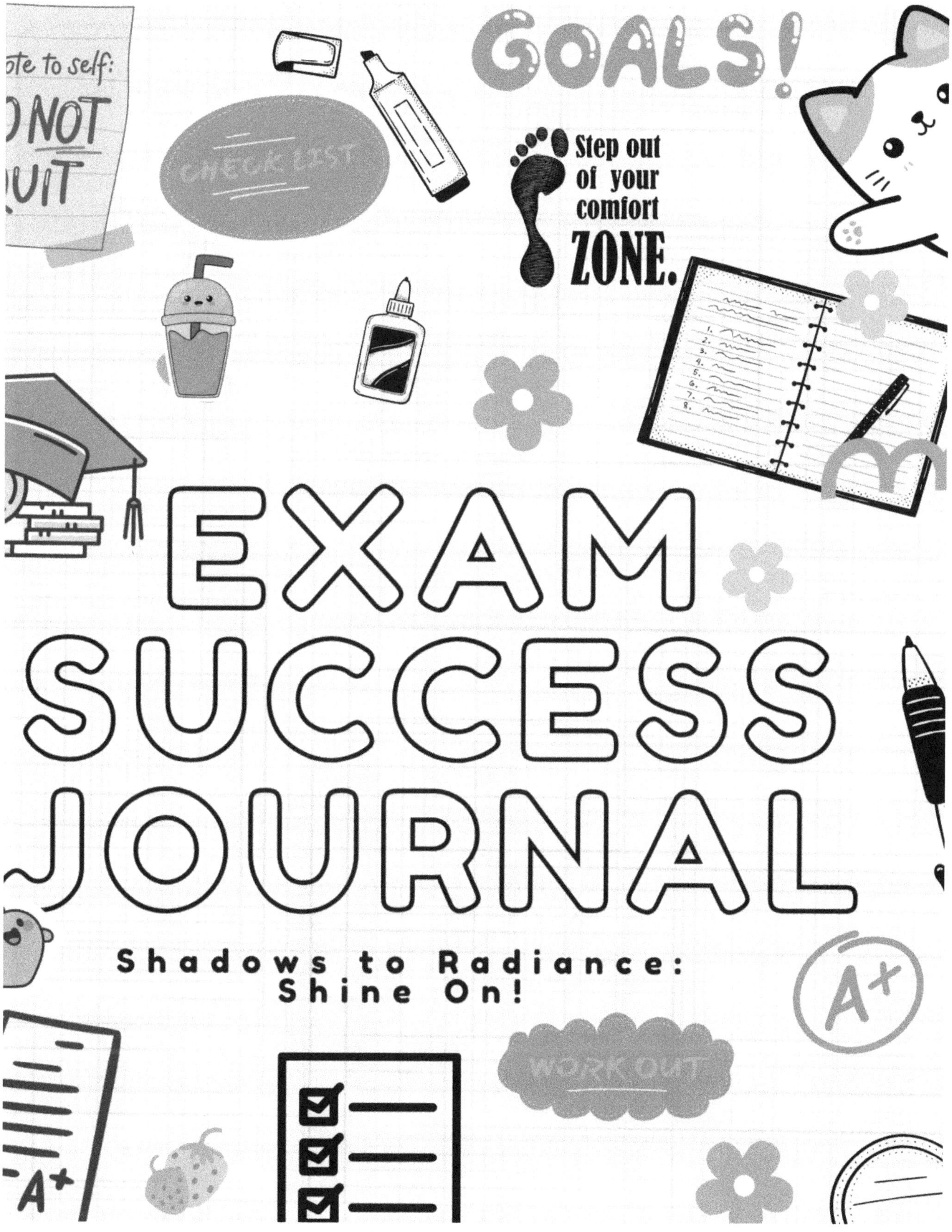
ote to self:
O NOT
QUIT
CHECK LIST
GOALS!
Step out
of your
comfort
ZONE.
WORK OUT
A+
A+

EXAM SUCCESS JOURNAL

Shadows to Radiance: Shine On!

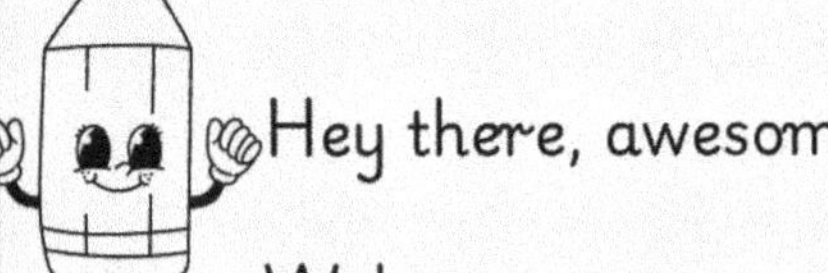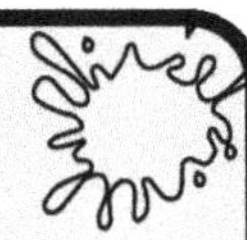

Hey there, awesome students!

Welcome to your very own Exam Success Journal! This little gem is your trusty sidekick for organizing your studies, managing your time like a pro, and pumping up your confidence as you gear up for those exams!

Inside, you'll discover nifty tips to kick fear to the curb, fun activities to sharpen your focus, and clever strategies to keep distractions at bay. Oh, and don't forget the breathing exercises for those quick focus boosts—think of it as your personal success playground!

Want to level up? Check out my special video by scanning the QR code below!

And here's a golden nugget: Before you hit the hay, tackle just one page of activities—it's a total game changer! You've got this, and I'm your biggest cheerleader!

Cheers,
Manisha Pathak
        (School Counselor, Positive Psychologist, and Nutritionist)

Dear Future

I AM READY!

Plan   Action   Achieve

Satrt with some Memory Hacks

Change Your Study Environment

Blink Rapidly Before Memorizing

Use 'Zeigarnik Effect'
Start learning something and leave in between, Start Again...

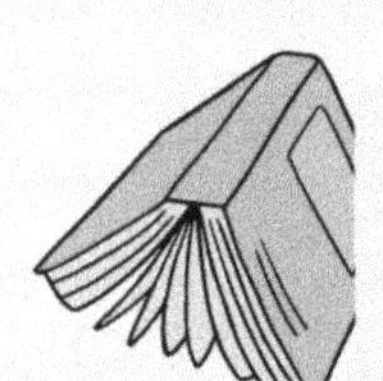

Squeeze your right fist before learning and your left fist before recalling; this activates the motor cortex, enhancing recall efficiency.

Practice 'TRATAK' by focusing intently on a candle flame without blinking your eyes.

Enjoy a Quick Power Nap

Present challenging concepts using a variety of fonts.

Exercise, Strech or Breathing Practices before Studies improves memory recall.

Satrt with some Memory Hacks

Understand CHUNKING..
Breaking down large information into smaller, manageable units. For example, instead of memorizing the number 123456789, you can chunk it into 123-456-789

Transform Study Information into Quizzes: Focus on What, When, and Why. Questions help improve memory retention. ?

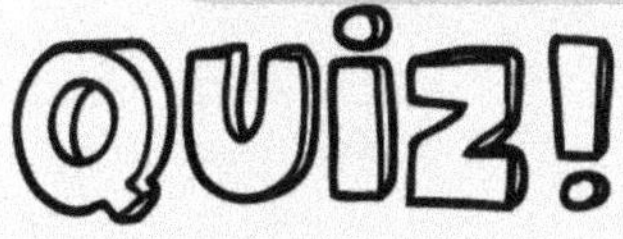

USE SENSES TO IMPROVE MEMORY

- Sing challenging formulas using a technique like "BHRAMRI," which involves humming.
- Visualize patterns and explore various recall systems that work best for you.

What pops into your noggin when you hear "Exam"? Grab those pens and doodle away! Let your imagination run wild!

Blueprint for My Epic Action Plan to Achieve Exam Success!

1. My Parents

My Epic Life Masterplan!

Imagine your exam results or dream goal achieved! Grab a pencil and doodle that victory like it's already yours!

DREAMS INTO REALITY

My outcome is in my hands, and I've achieved more than I anticipated. I can see the happiness radiating from everyone around me......

Celebrating your success! Who was there, and what were you all doing at that moment?

I have a feeling that I might forget things during the exam,
just like what happened in the last one.

Let's be creative and draw a vision board for your hobby or sports. Shhhh, it is a brain-boosting activity and will increase your memory power

The Potent "YET"

1. "This topic seems daunting now, yet I'm tackling it with determination!"
2. "I haven't perfected my study habits yet, but I'm developing a fitting strategy!"
3. "I'm not a master of this subject yet, but I'm gaining confidence with each step!"
4. "Exams may still intimidate me, yet I'm preparing to face them bravely!"

My Role Model !

Dear Student, Imagine the positive outcomes of your efforts—this can be empowering! Write a letter to your loved ones reflecting on your journey. Include what strategies worked and what didn't, along with the highs and lows you faced. Share your gratitude for the support you received and how you managed distractions and procrastination.
This exercise will help you articulate your experiences and reinforce positive thinking. Visualizing success truly makes a difference! Happy writing!

IMPORTANT REMINDERS

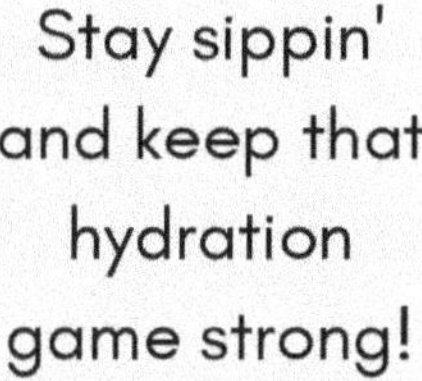

Stay sippin' and keep that hydration game strong!

SNOOZE Like a CHAMP at the right moment, and jot down your thoughts in a journal before sleeping!

Savor every bite of what mom is cooking!

Set those alarms and take a mini vacation from the screen!

Peer Study: Turn a brain-bursting topic into a fun teaching party!

Recall Game: Have a family member ask you random questions from any subject like a game show host!

Magical hours for challenging concepts!

Unleash those uplifting vibes with some positive affirmations!

Keep ALL your documents cozy in one happy plavce

Exam Day Checklist:
- Bring stationery
- Include approved calculators
- Have reference materials
- Follow device guidelines
- Arrive early

List your standout subjects—those where you excel and feel confident! These are your strengths ready to shine!

My Success mantra!

Set Your Calendar

Week 1   Date:

- Sun
- Mon
- Tue
- Wed
- Thu
- Fri
- Sat

Week 2   Date:

- Sun
- Mon
- Tue
- Wed
- Thu
- Fri
- Sat

<table><tr><td>Week 3</td><td>Date:</td></tr></table>

Sun

Mon

Tue

Wed

Thu

Fri

Sat

<table><tr><td>Week 4</td><td>Date:</td></tr></table>

Sun

Mon

Tue

Wed

Thu

Fri

Sat

<table><tr><td>Week 5</td><td>Date:</td></tr></table>

Sun

Mon

Tue

Wed

Thu

Fri

Sat

<table><tr><td>Week 6</td><td>Date:</td></tr></table>

Sun

Mon

Tue

Wed

Thu

Fri

Sat

Morning Timetable

Set up a daily routine and display it in a visible location to encourage consistent adherence. Start your day with a positive affirmation: "Today, I am going to..."

TO BE LIST

Resilient and Happy

Breaks

Take a deep breath and let it all out— LONG EXHALE TIME!

FRUIT-tastic TIMEOUT!

Make your bed

TIME to Doodle-Doodle-Do!

Kick back and chill with your favorite peeps!

TIDY up your space!

Today, I'm embracing my inner Zen master and feeling confident!

Welcome to the magic zone! This is your gateway to starting your day with positivity. Here's the secret:
Think of three things you're grateful for and say "thank you" like you just won the gratitude lottery! Say
positive words in your mind. With that thankfulness, envision how you want your day to unfold.

I'm grateful for the love from my amazing parents.

I appreciate my never-give-up attitude.

I love the refreshing morning air!

Take a moment to visualize your goals for today. Let the magic begin!

Each day is a blank canvas—set your intention and paint it with your dreams!"

Afternoon Timetable

Breaks

Cranking up the tunes!	JIGSAW of FUN!	MOM / DAD: The Rescuer!
Walk it out and count those steps!	FITNESS (Push-Up party!)	Give someone a big ol' shout-out!

Today, I'm set to achieve great productivity with focused energy!

Evening Timetable

Start your evening routine by reflecting on "WHAT WENT WELL TODAY." Write down at least three positive experiences to enhance your memory power.

Breaks

Chowing down on deliciously healthy goodness!	Breathe in that freshness!	Get your notes in line!
Journal Jotting!	Picking Joyful Vibes!	Make your bed!

what went well today!

Lunch was a total feast! Big thanks!   24.01.25

EXAM DATE SHEET 01

NAME :

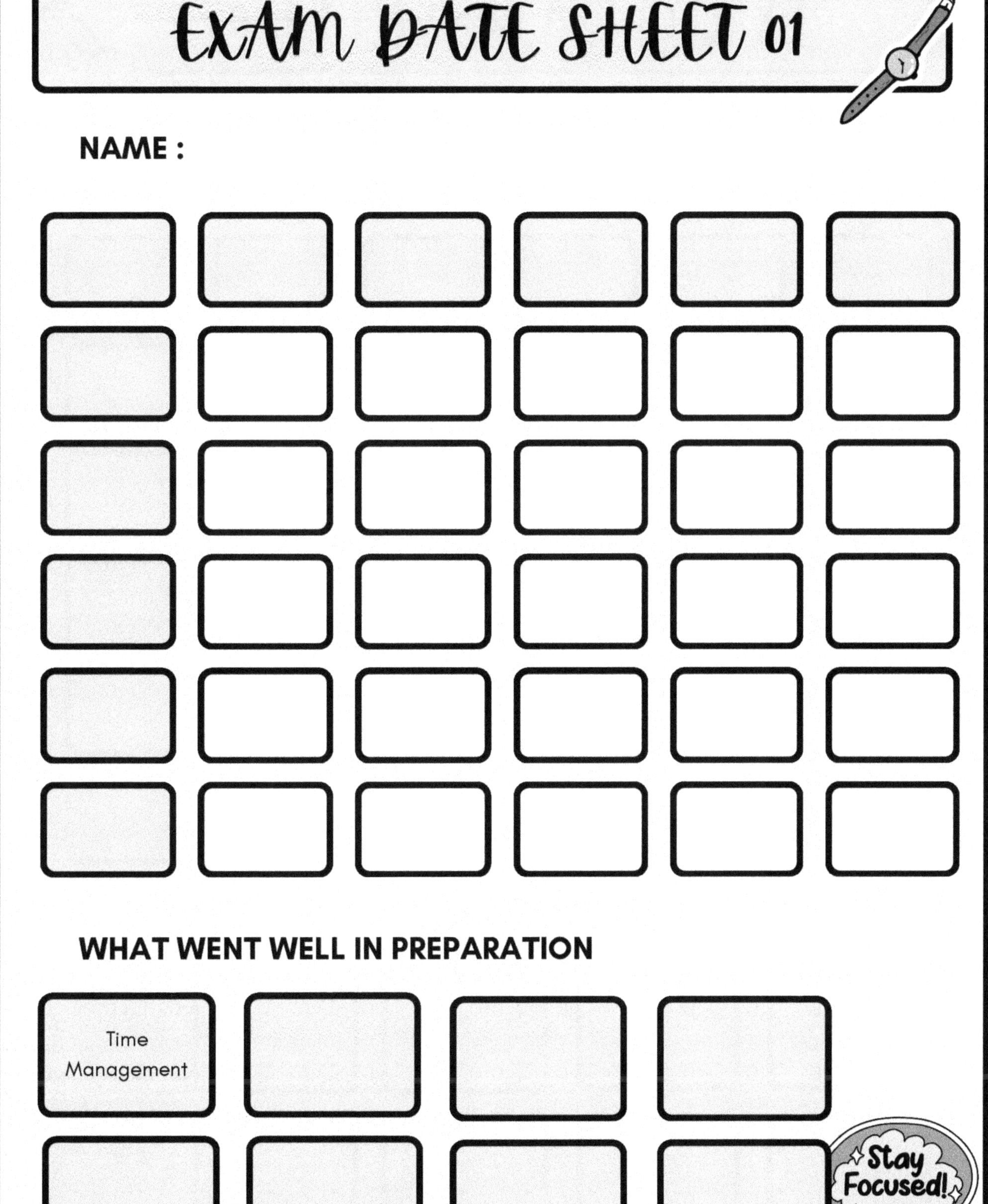

WHAT WENT WELL IN PREPARATION

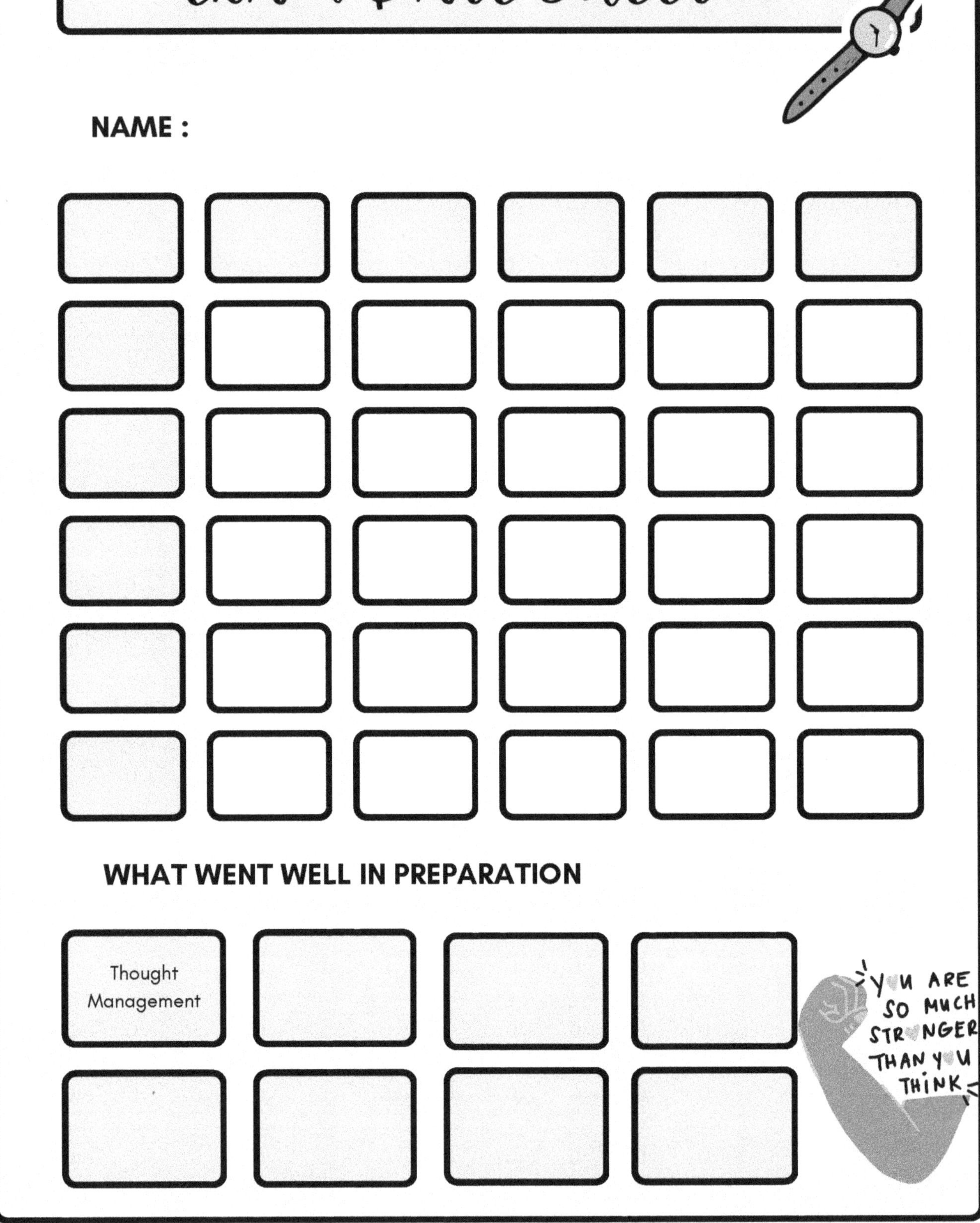

EXAM DATE SHEET 02

NAME :

WHAT WENT WELL IN PREPARATION

Thought Management

YOU ARE
SO MUCH
STRONGER
THAN YOU
THINK

Weekly Planner

WHIP UP A MASTER PLAN AND
HANG ON TIGHT!

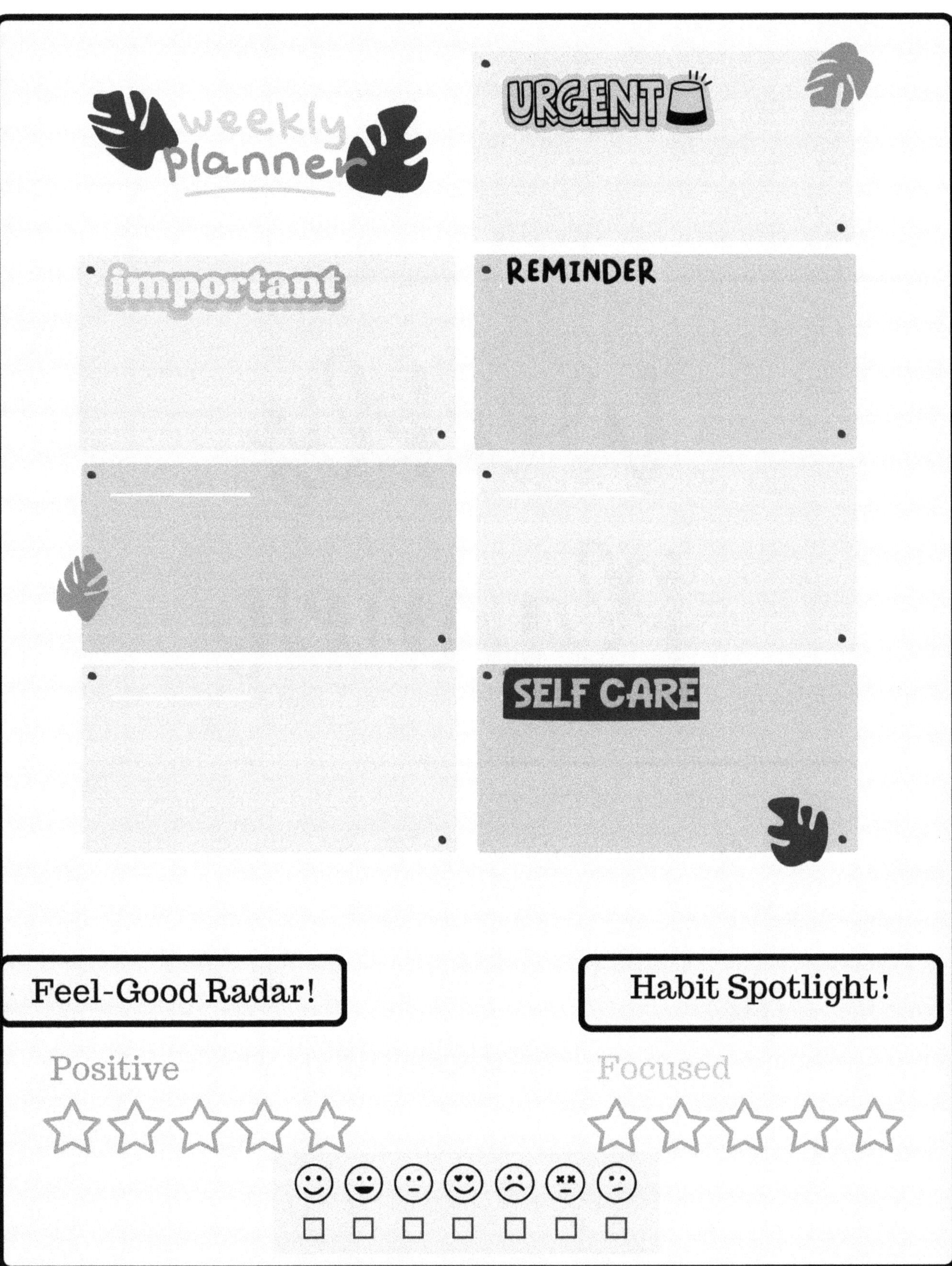

weekly planner
URGENT
important
REMINDER
SELF CARE
Feel-Good Radar!
Habit Spotlight!
Positive
Focused

My STAR TOPICS

Subject 01	02	03

04	05	Notes

my TOPIC NEEDS A LITTLE EXTRA TLC!

Subject 01

02

03

04

05

Notes

Sample Daily Planner!

Date
....

TO-DO LIST!
1. High Priority
2. Time-Sensitive

TO-BE LIST!
1. Be Productive
2. Stay Focused
3. Maintain Calm

ENERGY INVESTED
1. Time
2. Treasure
3. Health
4. Positive Mindset

NOTES

REMINDERS

DISCIPLINE OVER MOTIVATION

CHECKLIST
The list you dump
Yesterday for Tomorrow

DO IT!

Craft a guiding mantra for the day and inscribe it here.

My Daily Planner!

*When in doubt, just remember: even Einstein had to study...
and he had crazy hair to prove it!*

My Daily Planner!

Date

....

Hello! You promised to smile; it's the best exam strategy —
it confuses the questions!

My Daily Planner!

Date
....

Don't forget to eat those almond and nuts your mother soaked for you —
it's like brain food, but tastier and with fewer calories!

My Daily Planner!

Date

....

You're still a superhero — just because you're not wearing a cape
doesn't mean you can't save your grades!

My Daily Planner!

Date
....

Remember to switch off some lights or turn off the tap;
even the water wants a break!

REFLECT

TODAY'S PRIORITY LIST

WHAT WENT WELL

CHALLENGES

REMINDERS

SNEAKY DISTRACTIONS AND HABITS THAT HINDER YOUR AWESOME!

HABITS THAT ROCK YOUR WORLD!

Share
your
Thoughts

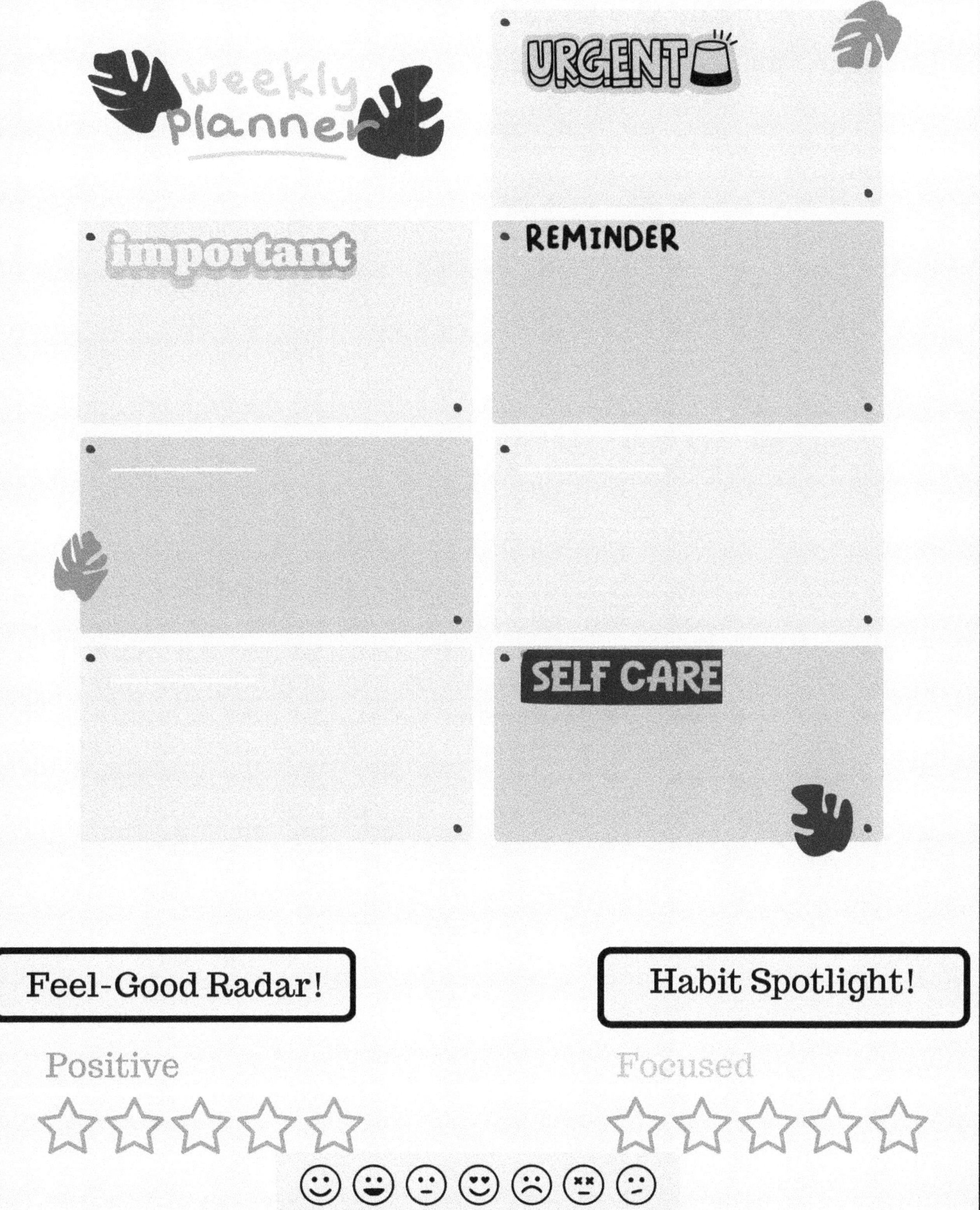

weekly planner
URGENT
important
REMINDER
SELF CARE
Feel-Good Radar!
Habit Spotlight!
Positive
Focused

My STAR TOPICS

Subject 01

02

03

04

05

Notes

My TOPIC NEEDS A LITTLE EXTRA TLC!

Subject 01

02

03

04

05

Notes

My Daily Planner!

Date

....

Keep a positivity jar filled with encouraging notes to remind you how awesome you are!

My Daily Planner!

Date
....

Hug your Parents/Pet. Snuggling up with your favorite people cranks up
your happiness meter and supercharges your brain!

My Daily Planner!

Date
....

Want a sprinkle of joy and a memory boost? Munch on tryptophan-packed treats like pumpkin seeds, yogurt, kidney beans, or salmon!

My Daily Planner!

Date
....

Create a cozy study nook—it's your success fortress filled with good vibes!

Whip up your own dazzling collection of brain-bending questions, toss it to your pals, and see who can crack the puzzles faster than a speeding bullet! Ready, set, challenge!

TODAY'S PRIORITY LIST

WHAT WENT WELL

CHALLENGES

REMINDERS

REFLECT

SNEAKY DISTRACTIONS AND HABITS THAT HINDER YOUR AWESOME!

HABITS THAT ROCK YOUR WORLD!

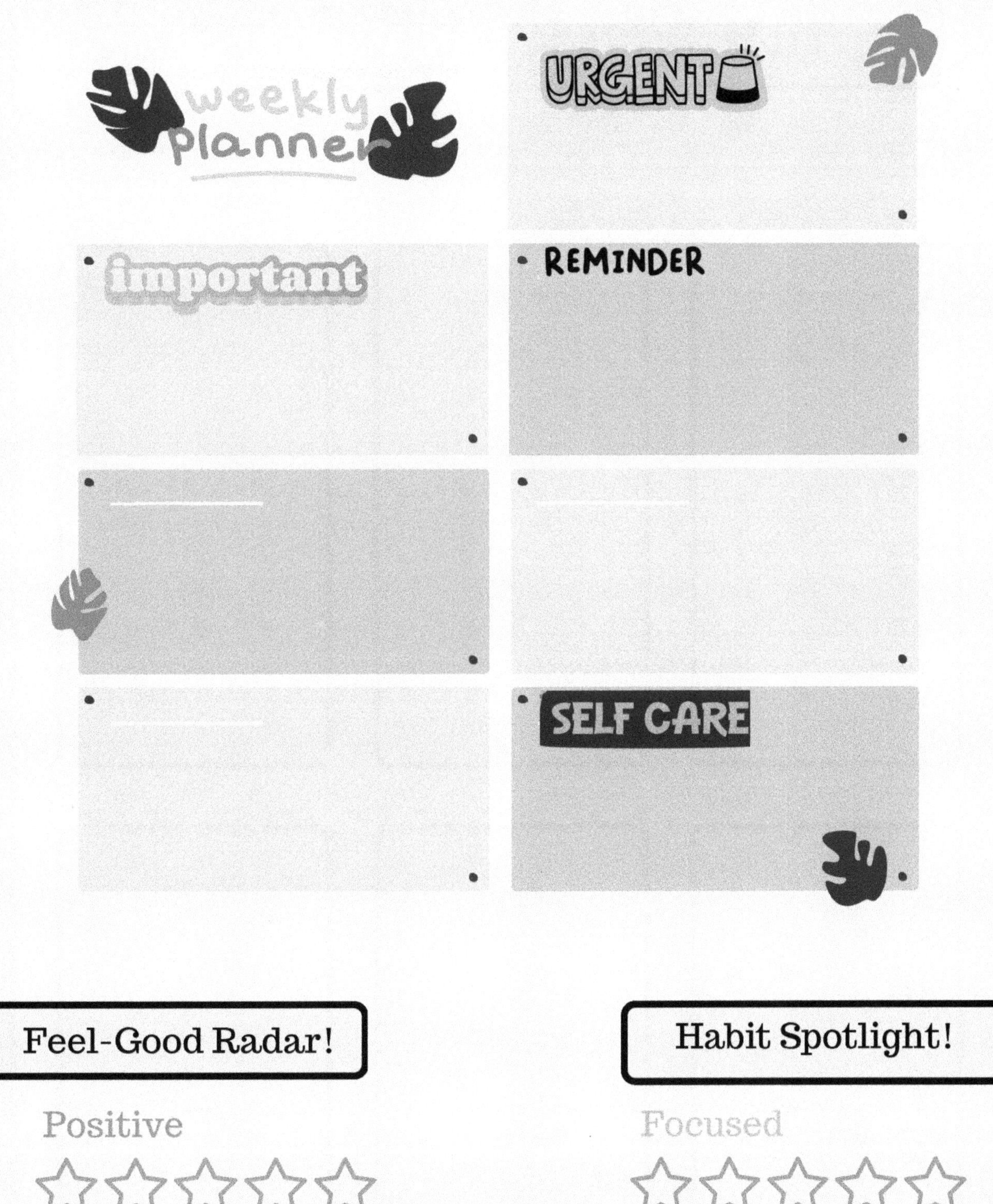

Feel-Good Radar!

Habit Spotlight!

Positive

Focused

MY STAR TOPICS

Subject 01	02	03
04	05	Notes

MY TOPIC NEEDS A LITTLE EXTRA TLC!

Subject 01

02

03

04

05

Notes

My Daily Planner!

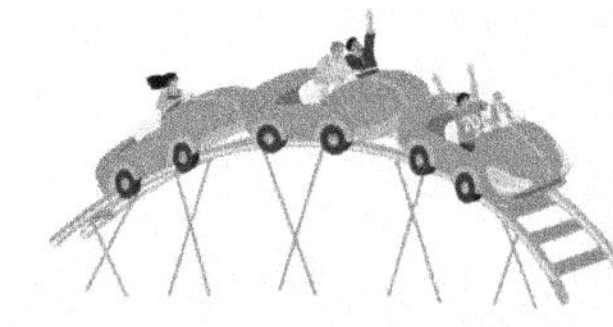

Visualize exam day as a rollercoaster ride—
you're in control, so enjoy!

My Daily Planner!

Date

....

Think of your brain as a superhero—
every study session is a power-up!

Date
....

Snack on colorful fruits and veggies—
they're brain boosters cheering you on!

Date
....

Remember, every genius was once a student!

My Daily Planner!

Date
....

Dance it out after mastering a topic—celebrate those little victories!

REFLECT

TODAY'S PRIORITY LIST

WHAT WENT WELL

CHALLENGES

REMINDERS

SNEAKY DISTRACTIONS AND HABITS THAT HINDER YOUR AWESOME!

HABITS THAT ROCK YOUR WORLD!

BE CREATIVE

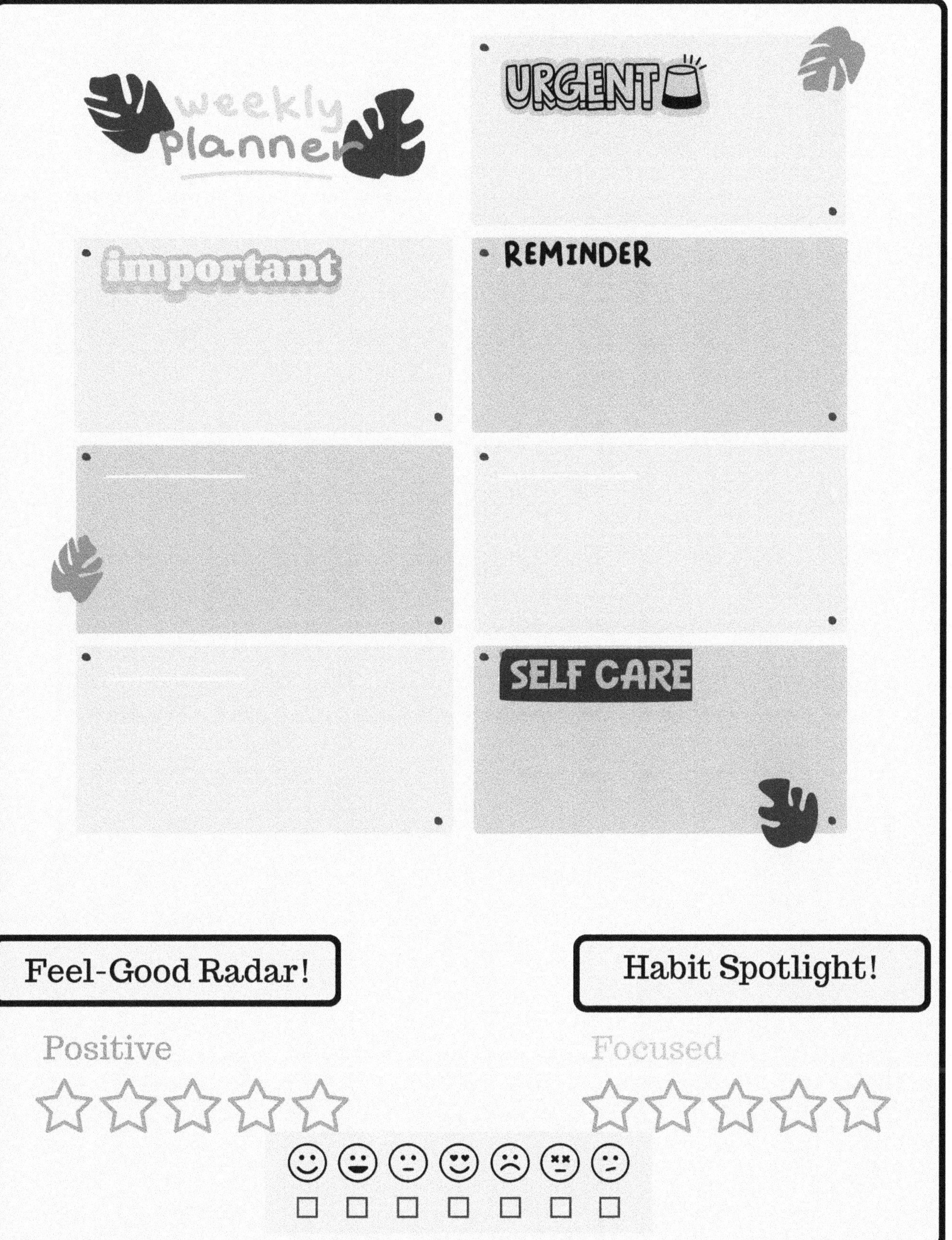

Feel-Good Radar!

Habit Spotlight!

Positive

Focused

MY STAR TOPICS

Subject 01	02	03
04	05	Notes

MY TOPIC NEEDS A LITTLE EXTRA TLC!

Subject 01

02

03

04

05

Notes

Date

....

Stay hydrated like a champion! Treat your water bottle as
your reliable companion on this exam journey!

STAY
HYDRATED

My Daily Planner!

Don't forget your ID card—
it's your golden ticket to the exam wonderland!

My Daily Planner!

Date
....

Take a deep breath and channel your inner Zen Master—
calm vibes only as you tackle those questions!

My Daily Planner!

Grab your favorite pen—
it's not just a tool; it's your magic wand for writing brilliance!

My Daily Planner!

Date

....

Celebrate like a champ after finishing a chapter—mini rewards rock!

TODAY'S PRIORITY LIST

WHAT WENT WELL

CHALLENGES

REMINDERS

REFLECT

SNEAKY DISTRACTIONS AND HABITS THAT HINDER YOUR AWESOME!

HABITS THAT ROCK YOUR WORLD!

BE CREATIVE

weekly planner

URGENT!

important

REMINDER

SELF CARE

Feel-Good Radar!

Habit Spotlight!

Positive

Focused

My STAR TOPICS

Subject 01

02

03

04

05

Notes

My Topic Needs a Little Extra TLC!

Subject 01

02

03

04

05

Notes

My Daily Planner!

Date

....

Set your exam timetable like a boss! It's your game plan, and you're the star player!

My Daily Planner!

Date

....

Take a deep breath and channel your inner zen master - calm vibes only as you tackle those questions!

My Daily Planner!

Date
....

Turn your study space into a cozy nook - Cushions, Sticky Notes
Mind Map and a sprinkle of fairy lights for extra inspiration!

My Daily Planner!

Date
....

Recognize and celebrate your achievements, whether they are significant or minor, as each step brings you closer to success - confetti is optional!

My Daily Planner!

Date
....

Prep like a pro! Lay out everything the night before so you can sleep like a baby and wake up ready to rock!

TODAY'S PRIORITY LIST

WHAT WENT WELL

CHALLENGES

REMINDERS

R
E
F
L
E
C
T

SNEAKY DISTRACTIONS AND HABITS
THAT HINDER YOUR AWESOME!

HABITS THAT ROCK
YOUR WORLD!

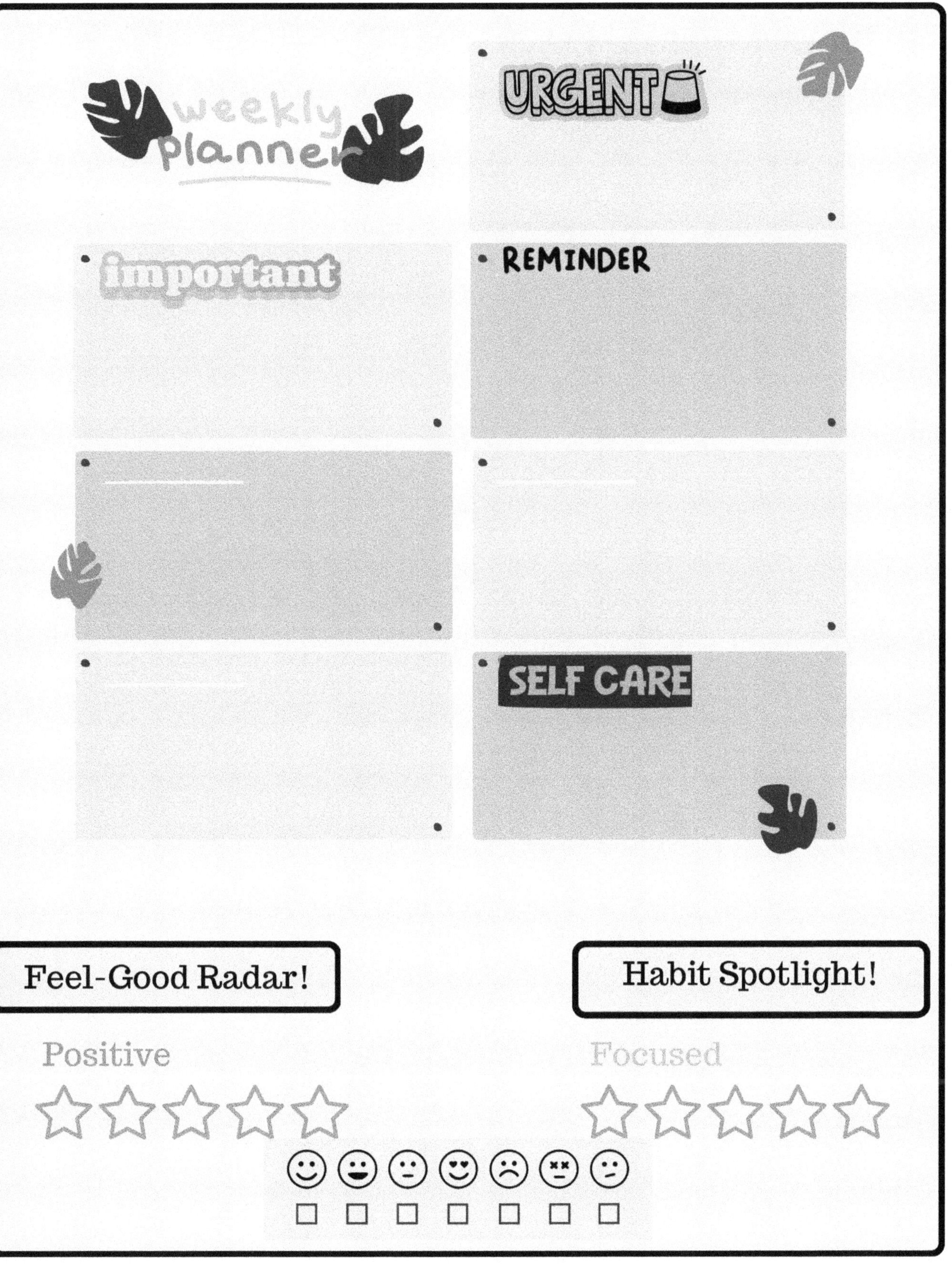

weekly planner
URGENT
important
REMINDER
SELF CARE
Feel-Good Radar!
Habit Spotlight!
Positive
Focused

My STAR TOPICS

Subject 01

02

03

04

05

Notes

my TOPIC NEEDS A LITTLE EXTRA TLC!

Subject 01

02

03

04

05

Notes

My Daily Planner!

Date
....

My Daily Planner!

Date

....

Slap motivational sticky notes around your study zone to keep the positivity flowing!

My Daily Planner!

Date
....

My Daily Planner!

Date
....

Try the Pomodoro technique: study hard for 25 minutes, then bust a move or shake
your body for 5 minutes of pure dance party!

My Daily Planner!

Date

....

Challange Yourself!

TODAY'S PRIORITY LIST
WHAT WENT WELL
REFLECT
CHALLENGES
REMINDERS
SNEAKY DISTRACTIONS AND HABITS THAT HINDER YOUR AWESOME!
HABITS THAT ROCK YOUR WORLD!

my STAR TOPICS

Subject 01

02

03

04

05

Notes

My Topic Needs A Little Extra TLC!

Subject 01

02

03

04

05

Notes

My Daily Planner!

Date
....

*Grab your rainbow of highlighters and transform your
study materials into a colorful masterpiece!*

Create a study playlist packed with your favorite feel-good tunes to keep the good vibes rolling!

My Daily Planner!

Date
....

Whip up a giant wall calendar and mark off your study days; there's nothing more satisfying than checking off those boxes!

My Daily Planner!

Date

....

Turn your notes into flashcards and challenge a friend to a trivia showdown —
who knew learning could be this fun?

My Daily Planner!

Date
....

Plan your meals ahead of time to dodge that last-minute junk food panic —
your brain will be doing a happy dance!

TODAY'S PRIORITY LIST

WHAT WENT WELL

CHALLENGES

REMINDERS

REFLECT

SNEAKY DISTRACTIONS AND HABITS THAT HINDER YOUR AWESOME!

HABITS THAT ROCK YOUR WORLD!

My STAR TOPICS

Subject 01

02

03

04

05

Notes

Subject 01

02

03

04

05

Notes

My Daily Planner!

Date
....

*Fuel up with snacks; your brain runs on healthy snacks —
but please, no gummy bears or chips!*

My Daily Planner!

Date

....

If you find a tough question, just pretend it's a monster —
and you're the bravest knight slaying it with your knowledge sword!

My Daily Planner!

Date
....

If you hear your stomach growl, it's probably just your brain asking for more probiotic — Have a glass of butter milk or sweet lime juice

Date
....

Take a dance break if you're feeling stuck; moving your body can
shake loose those tricky facts hiding in your brain!

My Daily Planner!

Date

....

Remember, every time you answer a question correctly,
a unicorn does a happy dance — and who doesn't want to see that?

TODAY'S PRIORITY LIST
WHAT WENT WELL
CHALLENGES
REMINDERS
REFLECT
SNEAKY DISTRACTIONS AND HABITS THAT HINDER YOUR AWESOME!
HABITS THAT ROCK YOUR WORLD!

BRAIN POWER UP TIME!

1 min

BRAIN POWER UP TIME!

Now summon forth the challenging subjects and inscribe them here.

Let your imagination run wild and doodle
away whatever pops into that brilliant brain
of yours!

Unleash your creativity and create
mandala magic with a compass!

Treasure Hunt: Get ready to unleash your inner explorer! Follow the clues, navigate your path, and sprint to the finish line where glorious treasure awaits! But here's the twist: no peeking at the instructions while you sketch your epic journey!

- Picture this: you're chillin' by the banyan tree when a guy with a snazzy blue umbrella pops up and asks you to pass it to a beggar.
- The beggar, feeling generous, hands you a packet of laddoos to take to the temple, and you score some juicy mangoes in return.
- After devouring those delightful mangoes, you make a dramatic U-turn and opt for the flyover route, leading you to a picturesque garden by the lake.
- And just when you think it can't get better, you plant a seed, dig into the soil, and—boom!—you discover a treasure pot! Let the adventure begin!

UNLEASH YOUR INNER PUZZLE MASTER WITH SUDOKU!

Sudoku #1

		3	9			5		
		7	1			4		
					7	3		
			6	4				
8			2	3		9		
						1		
3	1			9				5
	5	8	3					4
							1	3

Sudoku #2

6				1	7			
	3	8	9	4				
				2			4	
5		1	3		8		2	9
		3		2		1		
9	2		1					
1	9	6			3		8	4
4						7		
	5	7	2					1

Solution #1

1	2	3	9	6	4	5	7	8
5	8	7	1	2	3	4	6	9
4	9	6	5	8	7	3	2	1
2	3	1	6	4	9	8	5	7
8	7	5	2	3	1	9	4	6
9	6	4	8	7	5	1	3	2
3	1	2	4	9	6	7	8	5
7	5	8	3	1	2	6	9	4
6	4	9	7	5	8	2	1	3

Solution #2

6	4	9	5	1	7	8	3	2
2	3	8	9	4	6	5	1	7
7	1	5	8	3	2	9	4	6
5	6	1	3	7	8	4	2	9
8	7	3	4	2	9	1	6	5
9	2	4	1	6	5	3	7	8
1	9	6	7	5	3	2	8	4
4	8	2	6	9	1	7	5	3
3	5	7	2	8	4	6	9	1

Breathe Your Way to Exam Victory!

3 min

Maintain a straight posture and exhale for a count of four through your mouth, then inhale gently through your nose.

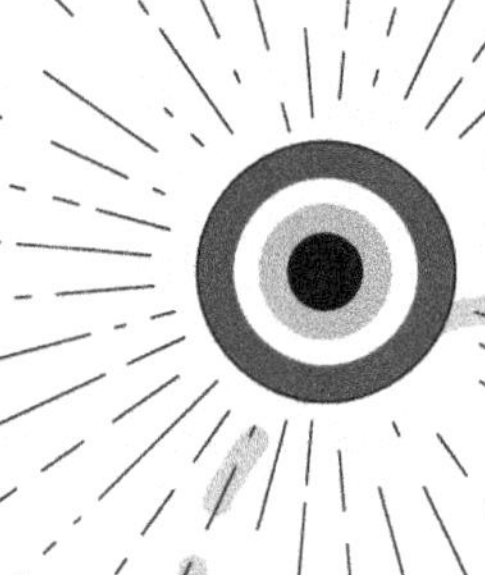

Imagine your Vision Board or Goals. Picture yourself having accomplished them, and envision your parents celebrating your success. Allow yourself to fully experience the feelings that come with this achievement.

Inhale deeply, hold your breath for four seconds, then gently exhale while opening your eyes.

Engage in simple, natural breathing by concentrating on your nostrils. Take a moment to feel the air as you breathe. Sit comfortably, then stand up to drink a little water.

Hey there!

We hope you had a blast with this journal! Don't keep the fun to yourself—share it with your pals and drop us a review to help us sprinkle some magic on our next edition. Huge thanks to all the fabulous parents for this awesome gift! Wishing you all the luck in your exams and a future that shines brighter than a supernova! Got questions? Hit us up at manishapathak.com!

Best wishes

Sanjeevani Wellness Publication